THE EARTH'S RESOURCES

Steve Parker

HODDER
Wayland

an imprint of Hodder Children's Books

SCIENCE FACT FILES

CRIMINAL INVESTIGATION • COMMUNICATIONS
THE EARTH'S RESOURCES • ELECTRICITY AND MAGNETISM
FORCES AND MOTION • GENETICS
THE HUMAN BODY • LIGHT AND SOUND
THE SOLAR SYSTEM • WEATHER

Produced by Roger Coote Publishing
Gissing's Farm, Fressingfield
Suffolk IP21 5SH

First published in 2000 by Hodder Wayland
An imprint of Hodder Children's Books
This paperback edition published in 2001
Reprinted in 2002
Text copyright © 2000 Hodder Wayland
Volume copyright © 2000 Hodder Wayland

Design and typesetting	Jane Hawkins
Editor	Sarah Doughty
Picture Researcher	Lynda Lines
Illustrator	Alex Pang

Endpaper picture: A geothermal power plant in Iceland
Title page picture: A solar furnace

We are grateful to the following for permission to reproduce photographs:
MPM/Digital Vision front cover top, front cover bottom, front endpapers, 5, 9, 10, 11 left, 16, 21 bottom, 22 top, 23, 27 left, 39 top, 40 bottom, 41; Photri front cover main image; Science and Society Picture Library/Science Museum 21 top, 37 bottom; Science Photo Library 11 right (Russ Munn/AGS), 12 top (Simon Fraser), 14 top (Geco UK), 14 bottom (Geospace), 17 left (Chris Knapton), 19 (Rosenfeld Images Ltd), 22 bottom (AT&T Bell Labs/Peter Arnold Inc), 24 top (Joe Pasieka), 25 (Geco UK), 27 right (Peter Menzel), 29 bottom (Dr Jeremy Burgess), 31 top (Crown Copyright/Health & Safety Laboratory), 32 top (Jim Gipe/Agstock), 33 (William Ervin), 34 bottom (Maximilian Stock Ltd), 35 (Alex Bartel), 36 (Martin Bond), 38 (Martin Bond), 40 top (Martin Bond), 42 (Martin Bond), 43 top (Martin Bond), 43 bottom (Simon Fraser); Still Pictures 32 bottom (John Isaac), 37 top (Julio Etchart); Stock Market 12 bottom; Stone 8 top (Rex A Butcher), 8 bottom (Greg Proost), 13 (John Lawrence), 15 (Lester Lefkowitz), 17 right (Charles Thatcher), 18 (Steve Taylor), 26 (Mark A Leman), 29 top (Bob Thomason), 31 bottom (Bruce Ando), 34 top (Ragnar Sigurdsson).

The statistics given in this book are the most up to date available at
the time of going to press.

Printed in Hong Kong by Wing King Tong

A CIP catalogue record for this book is available from the British Library

ISBN 0 7500 2722 3

Hodder Children's Books
A division of Hodder Headline Limited
338 Euston Road, London NW1 3BH

CONTENTS

The words that are explained in the glossary are printed
in **bold** the first time they are mentioned in the text.

WHAT ARE RESOURCES?

In a giant supermarket you can buy most of life's needs. There are vital items such as foods, drinks and clothes. There are also useful goods such as washing machines, bicycles and furniture, and the latest gadgets such as mobile phones and laptop computers. The supermarket is so vast that you cannot see the other end. It seems that the supplies of goods and products are endless. But are they? And where do they all come from?

They come from our home planet – Earth. It provides the raw materials, substances and sources of energy that people need or use in their daily lives. These are called Earth's natural resources and they are obtained from above, on and within our planet.

Natural resources

Some natural resources are essential for survival. They include the air we breathe, the food we eat and the water we drink.

Other natural resources are not vital for survival. But they help to make people's lives more comfortable and convenient. For example, oil (crude oil or petroleum) is obtained from Earth and made into fuels such as petrol for our cars and trucks.

Every single item in this superstore has been manufactured from Earth's natural resources – goods for sale, shelves, lighting and even the building itself.

EARLY RESOURCE-USERS

People, like animals and plants, have always relied on Earth's basic natural resources of air, food and water. But about two million years ago, people began to change other natural objects for their own use, which is something very few animals do. They chipped pieces of flint and other rocks to produce sharp edges for cutting. Gradually they altered natural objects more to make hand axes, spears, arrows and a widening range of weapons and tools.

By half a million years ago early people were using another type of natural resource – fire. Its flames gave off energy as light and heat. The light energy allowed people to see in the dark. The heat energy kept them warm and enabled them to cook food.

Billions are spent each year on finding more oil, one of the most important and widely used natural resources, in remote places.

Renewable resources

Some natural resources are renewable. They are continually being made or reformed through natural processes. For example, certain farm crops grow each year without special fertilizers or weedkillers. There is a continuing supply of energy from wind. Water supplies are regularly renewed by rain, as part of Earth's natural water cycle (see page 10).

Intensive farming of food crops, one of our basic natural resources, is a global industry that in turn relies on other resources, such as fuel.

Non-renewable resources

Supplies of non-renewable resources are not replaced by nature as quickly as they are used. One of the main examples is oil. People have used vast amounts of oil in the past 100 or so years. But it took millions of years for this oil to form by natural processes. Today's rate of oil use is much greater than the rate of oil formation.

This book describes the wide range of natural resources provided by Earth, and how people use them. It also shows how using Earth's resources can cause great problems such as waste and pollution, and how some non-renewable resources are in danger of running out because people are using them too quickly.

NATURAL RESOURCES FOR LIFE

Two natural resources essential for life are air and water – not only for people, but for animals and plants, too. Air forms an invisible blanket around Earth called the atmosphere. It becomes thinner with height and fades away to nothing about 1,000 kilometres above Earth's surface.

The atmosphere is a mixture of several gases. The most important are needed for life – oxygen, the invisible gaseous form of water called water vapour, and carbon dioxide. In addition, moving air in the atmosphere – called wind – is one source of renewable energy (see page 38).

Vital oxygen

Living things, or organisms, need oxygen to survive. This gas is vital for respiration, the process in which energy is released from food. This energy is needed for breathing, moving, eating and other activities of life. Oxygen forms about one-fifth of the atmosphere. People obtain it by breathing air into their lungs. During respiration some oxygen in the air is converted into carbon dioxide and is breathed out.

The water cycle

Water is a natural resource that is needed by all living things. Water is not made or destroyed on Earth. The same water goes round and round on countless journeys that form the water cycle. The Sun's warmth heats water in seas and lakes and evaporates it, changing it into water vapour.

Plants are vital as food for ourselves and animals. But they rely on a resource which does not come from Earth – the Sun's light energy.

The vapour rises in air, where it becomes cooler with height. It condenses or turns back into tiny drops of liquid water. The drops form clouds and eventually fall back to Earth as rain, hail and snow. Some of the rain water soaks into the soil, runs into streams and rivers, then collects in lakes and seas. As this water evaporates the cycle continues. Plants and animals take in and give out water in different ways, but all need continuing supplies.

How the water cycle works

Evaporation from sea

Plants give out water

Rivers flow into sea

Sea

Clouds (water vapour)

Rain, hail and snow fall to Earth

Water runs into rivers

In the water cycle, the same water moves around in liquid form, as a gas (invisible water vapour) and a solid (frozen ice and snow).

Carbon dioxide

Carbon dioxide gas forms only a tiny amount of the atmosphere (see Fact File), but it is vital for plants. They take in carbon dioxide and water and join them together using the energy they capture from sunlight, to form energy-rich sugars. Plants use the sugars as food. This process by which plants make their food is called **photosynthesis**. Oxygen is released into the air as a by-product of photosynthesis.

Photosynthesis changes carbon dioxide to oxygen. Respiration, as explained above, does the opposite. These two life processes help to maintain the balance of gases in the atmosphere. In effect, plants refresh the air with oxygen. However in recent years the balance of gases in the atmosphere has been upset by many human activities causing pollution (see page 15).

FACT FILE

GASES IN AIR
• Normal air contains the following main gases in these proportions:

Nitrogen	78 per cent
Oxygen	21 per cent
Argon	0.9 per cent
Carbon dioxide	0.03 per cent
Neon	0.002 per cent

• Other gases occur in air in even smaller amounts, including helium, krypton, xenon and ozone.
• The amount of water vapour in air, called humidity, varies greatly with the weather and the region of Earth. Air with low humidity has little water vapour and feels 'dry'. Air with high humidity has lots of water vapour and feels 'sticky' or 'clammy'.

Plants such as soya provide food and useful products, and also maintain the natural gases in the atmosphere to keep the air 'fresh'.

SOIL AS A NATURAL RESOURCE

When trees are taken away for timber or to create grazing land, soil which took centuries to form can be washed away in just a few hours.

A farmer spreading a chemical fertilizer on the land. Fertilizers help to keep soil fertile by replacing minerals and nutrients used up by plants as they grow.

Soil may seem dull, uninteresting or even 'dirty'. But without soil, plants could not grow. There would be no woodlands or wildlife, and no farm crops and animals. Soil is a very precious natural resource.

What is soil?

Soil is a complex mixture of many substances. It contains small fragments of minerals from rocks which have been worn down by heat, cold, rain, ice, snow and the other forces of nature – a process called weathering.

Soil also contains the remains of living things and their parts and products, such as plant leaves and animal droppings. Once these materials fall to the ground they decay and are broken down. The result is a brown, **fertile** layer of soil called **humus**. It contains many minerals and **nutrients**. The remains decay further into smaller pieces and may pass deeper into the soil. Plants eventually take in the minerals and nutrients through their roots and use them for new growth. In this way, soil helps to naturally **recycle** minerals and other substances through the environment.

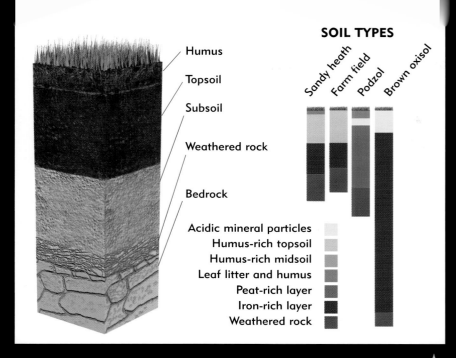

Humus

Topsoil

Subsoil

Weathered rock

Bedrock

Sandy heath
Farm field
Podzol
Brown oxisol

Acidic mineral particles
Humus-rich topsoil
Humus-rich midsoil
Leaf litter and humus
Peat-rich layer
Iron-rich layer
Weathered rock

Soil is divided into layers: humus, topsoil, subsoil and weathered rock. In different soil types, these layers contain varying depths of different materials.

FACT FILE

TYPES OF SOIL

The average sizes of the mineral particles and rock fragments in soil greatly affect the type of soil and the plants it supports.
• A sandy soil has relatively large particles, about 2 to 0.2 millimetres across. Water drains easily between them so sandy soils are light and dry.
• Clay particles are much smaller, less than 0.004 millimetres across. They pack closely together and trap water to make the soil heavy and waterlogged.

Living soil

A rich or fertile soil teems with life such as worms, grubs, mites and other small creatures. Larger animals, such as rabbits, prairie dogs and wombats, may make their burrows in the ground. There are also the roots of plants, the spreading threads of fungi (moulds and mushrooms), and billions of **microbes** such as bacteria. The tunnelling activity of animals such as earthworms allows air and water to spread easily through the soil and improve its fertility.

Conserving soil

The roots of trees and other plants help to prevent soil from being washed away by heavy rain or blown away in high winds. In some areas, trees are cut down or burned to clear land for other uses. In the process, their roots are destroyed. Without the roots, the soil becomes loose and is easily washed away by

rain, or carried away by wind. When this happens, the land loses its soil cover. Rivers are choked as they fill up with the resulting mud. A similar problem happens if too many crops are grown too often in soil. They use up its minerals and nutrients and the soil becomes thin and loose.

If deep, rich soil is lost from an area, it may take between 50 and 100 years for just 2–3 centimetres of new soil to form. So it is vital to conserve this precious natural resource, both for people and for wildlife.

In natural habitats, nutrients taken from the ground by plants are returned as fallen leaves, twigs, flowers and fruits.

ROCK AND MINERAL RESOURCES

The rocks that make up the hard outer layer, or crust, of Earth are natural resources. Rocks are generally hard, solid masses formed by natural processes and made of minerals. Minerals are also usually solid, formed by natural processes, and each has a definite chemical make-up. For example the mineral silica is made of the **elements** silicon and oxygen. Sand grains on the beach are made of quartz, a form of silica. Sand grains which have been naturally pressed and cemented together form the rock sandstone.

Wide-ranging uses

The mineral quartz and the rock sandstone are valuable natural resources with many different uses. Sand is a raw material in the manufacture of glass. It is also mixed with cement to make mortar for fixing together bricks and blocks and to make concrete for the construction industry. Sandstone is cut and shaped into blocks, bricks and slabs for building and is sometimes used for road-building.

People use hundreds of other rocks and minerals as natural resources, both in their raw form, and also to obtain substances such as **metals** and precious **gems** from them, as explained on the following pages.

Surveying the site

Rocks are usually obtained by quarrying and minerals by mining (see page 16). These processes are often expensive and normally require large industrial machinery. Before mining or quarrying begins, geologists (scientists who study rocks, minerals and other aspects of Earth) usually survey a site to make sure it will yield enough material to be worth the expense.

Computer-aided surveys use shock waves or seismic waves to build up a three-dimensional image of mineral resources deep under the ground.

Photographs taken by Landsat satellites may reveal new resources such as ore rocks or water. This view shows the Himalaya mountains.

A survey may begin with detailed pictures taken from satellites that orbit Earth. These pictures give an overview of the area. A plane may then fly over the region for a closer look. It may take photographs and also use instruments that measure tiny variations in Earth's natural magnetic field and its pull of gravity. An area of iron-containing rocks, for example, distorts Earth's magnetic field. Obtaining information like this at a distance, such as from satellites and planes, is called remote sensing.

Surveyors then visit the site, take rock samples at the surface and perhaps use a drilling rig to obtain deeper rocks for study. They may also carry out test explosions, almost like creating mini-earthquakes. Different types of rocks carry the shock (seismic) waves of an explosion in different ways.

 **FUTURE FILE**

A NEW THREAT

In the past, building blocks, statues, carvings, tombstones and other items made from hard rocks, such as granite, lasted for hundreds of years. Today they face the threat of **acid rain** due to air pollution. Gases in the exhaust fumes from vehicles and electricity generating stations, rise into the air and combine with the tiny water drops which form clouds and rain. They turn the rain into an acid. This falls to Earth and eats away the stone. Look at the stone structures in your neighbourhood. Are they being worn away by acid rain and other forms of pollution?

This stone sculpture in a cemetery in New York City, USA has been damaged by acid rain.

15

QUARRYING AND MINING

Rocks are obtained by quarrying. A quarry is basically a large hole where the rocks are at or just beneath the surface. Sometimes explosives are used to break huge blocks of hard rock, such as granite, into smaller pieces which can be handled or transported. Shot holes are drilled for sticks of dynamite or a similar explosive. Then everyone moves to a safe place as the siren warns of the blast to come. Suitable blocks are cut from the different-sized chunks that result.

Softer rocks may be dug out using boring or excavating machines. Or they may be cut directly from the ground using special saws and cutters. Their blades are tipped with extremely hard substances such as diamond or the metal tungsten.

These miners are drilling a hole in a mine wall. Detonating explosives in the hole will break up the rock.

Mining

A mine is usually a deeper pit, tunnel or excavation used to obtain minerals from under the ground. However minerals may be obtained at or near the surface by **open-cast mining** which is similar to quarrying. (Coal mining is a specialized form of mining, see page 30.)

Miners, like quarriers, use a variety of methods to dig up or excavate minerals. They include the drill-and-blast method with explosives, and large rotating drill bits or circular saws, as described above. In some mines the workers use hand-held power tools such as jackhammers. The minerals obtained are transported out of the mine by conveyor belts or by small rail wagons driven by electric motors or diesel engines.

A tunnel or shaft in a mine must be supported to prevent cave-ins. In some cases the surrounding rock is so hard that it naturally supports itself. Timber or metal posts and beams can also be fitted against the wall, as the mining tunnel or chamber lengthens.

FACT FILE

POTTERY AND CERAMICS

• Clay and minerals obtained from clay are used for various types of pottery. The damp clay is moulded and shaped, then fired – heated in an oven or kiln to make it hard.

• Clay-based minerals are also blended with substances such as metals or plastics to make modern high-technology ceramics. These are incredibly hard and withstand great temperatures. They are used in jet engines, on the cutting edges of drills and saws, and to make bullet-proof clothing.

Ceramic insulators look like stacks of large plates. They prevent electricity leaking from the cable into the metal pylon and down into the ground.

Minerals for construction

Huge amounts of rocks and minerals are used by the construction industry. Bricks and tiles are made from minerals in clays which are mixed and put into moulds or sliced as block shapes. They are hardened by heat in a special oven, or kiln, in a process called firing.

Cement is vital in construction. It is used in concrete and in the paste-like mortar that holds bricks together. Cement is made from calcium-rich rocks such as chalk or limestone, and rocks such as shale that are rich in alumina and silica minerals. These are ground, mixed and heated in a kiln at about 1,350°C to form lumps called clinker. The clinker is ground and mixed with small amounts of minerals such as gypsum to produce the fine grey powder, cement. World-wide, more than 1,000 million tonnes of cement are produced yearly.

Making cement is a highly technical process controlled from a central room. Sensors measure the amounts of raw materials in the mix.

PRECIOUS STONES

The hardest natural mineral on Earth is diamond. It is also one of the most valuable natural resources. Diamonds are used widely in industry because of their hardness, for marking, cutting, grinding and polishing. They are also treasured as gems because they are very rare, and when they are cut and polished they shine with an incredible sparkling 'fire' of colours.

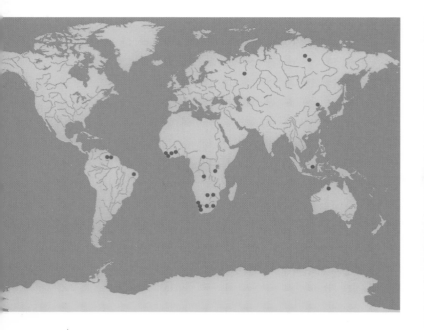

The main sources of the world's diamonds are South Africa and Russia. There are also mines in central and West Africa, Australia, South America and Asia.

Mineral colours

Diamond is called a precious stone because it is valuable and found as lumps in the ground, like stones. There are many other precious stones such as sapphires, rubies and emeralds. They are valued for their shining brilliance, beautiful colours, hardness and rarity.

Often the colour of a precious stone is due to tiny amounts of a natural chemical substance or element contained within it. For example, the mineral corundum contains the elements aluminium and oxygen, combined as aluminium oxide.

This small gem, a diamond, was once a dull, irregular-shaped lump in the ground. A gem-cutter shapes and polishes each 'stone' individually.

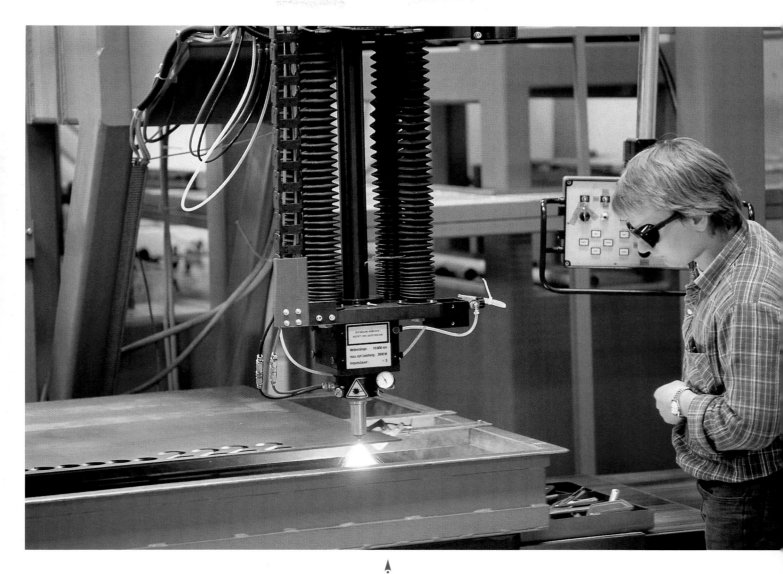

In clear forms of corundum tiny amounts of a third element, the metal chromium, produce the red colour of the precious stone ruby. The same mineral but with tiny amounts of the metals iron and titanium instead produce the blue precious stone sapphire.

Some types of lasers use precious minerals, including gems such as ruby, to generate their intense, high-energy, pure-colour beams of light.

Cut and polished

Most precious stones are dug out of mines. Huge amounts of rocks must be excavated and sorted to yield tiny amounts of the precious stones. This is the main reason they are so costly. On average, a volume of rock equivalent to 20 family houses must be mined to obtain one pea-sized diamond. The 'rough' or 'native' precious stone, as dug from the ground, is usually lumpy and frosty-looking. It takes much time and skill to cut and polish it to make a jewel or gem that shows off its colour and reflects light in the best way.

High-tech jewels

Precious stones are used not only in jewellery but in high-technology equipment. The very first laser, made in 1960, used a ruby to make the light reflect many times and gain energy. Tiny diamonds that are too small for rings or necklaces are used to tip cutters, drill bits and saw teeth. Artificial diamonds for industrial use have been produced since the 1950s. Some are high enough in quality to be real gems – but they often cost more to make than mining natural diamonds.

INDUSTRIAL METALS

Some of the most common, familiar and useful of Earth's natural resources are metals. These are minerals which are pure chemical substances or elements, such as iron, copper, tin, lead, aluminium and zinc. Most metals are hard, shiny and tough, and carry heat and electricity well. Many are ductile, which means they can be drawn out into long, thin wires, or malleable, which means they can be hammered or beaten into shapes such as thin sheets.

Metals can occur naturally in pure form, such as gold nuggets which have been found lying on the ground. But most metals occur joined or linked to other elements, as compounds. These compounds are spread through the rocks of Earth's crust. Rocks which contain enough of a metal to make mining and extraction worthwhile are known as metal ores.

The Ages of Metals

Metals have been so important during human history that time periods have been named after them. From about 6,500 years ago, in parts of the world such as the Middle East, people learned how to heat rocks containing the metals copper and tin, to obtain these metals and mix them together. The mixture or alloy of copper and tin is called bronze, so this time is known as the Bronze Age. Then about 3,500 years ago people learned how to obtain pure iron from ores, and this began the Iron Age.

Iron and steel

The most widely used metal is iron. This is partly because it is the basis for the most common metal alloy – steel – which is iron mixed with small amounts of carbon and other substances.

Iron is the fourth most common chemical element in Earth's crust. Rocks which contain enough iron for extraction are called iron ores. They are heated to 1,000°C in a huge chimney-like blast furnace with limestone and coke (made by controlled burning of coal). Blasts of very hot air are blown through the mixture. The result is pig iron which still has some impurities. Most of this is converted into steel by further heating, blowing gases through it and adding other substances.

Steel has hundreds of industrial uses, from making railway lines and locomotives to girders in bridges and skyscrapers. Steel sheet forms car bodies and the metal casings of washing machines and similar appliances.

How steel is made

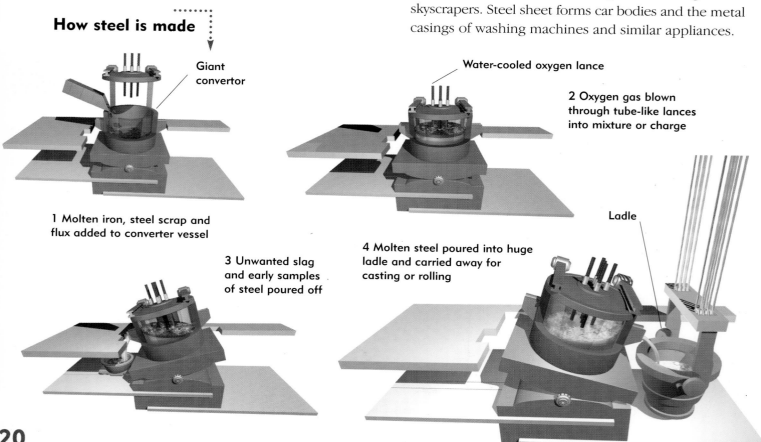

Giant convertor

Water-cooled oxygen lance

2 Oxygen gas blown through tube-like lances into mixture or charge

Ladle

1 Molten iron, steel scrap and flux added to converter vessel

3 Unwanted slag and early samples of steel poured off

4 Molten steel poured into huge ladle and carried away for casting or rolling

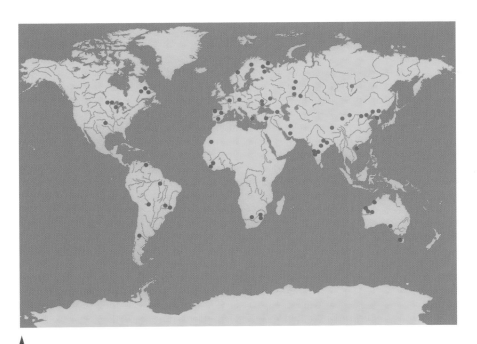

The main sites of iron ore rocks in the world.

This axe-head and two chisel-like implements from Hungary are made of bronze – one of the first metal alloys used by people.

The most plentiful metal in Earth's crust, aluminium, is strong yet extremely light and rarely corrodes. It has a huge variety of uses, from saucepans to jumbo jets.

Electric motors, pumps and many other machines contain different types of steels. Cutlery, paper clips, scissors and many other household objects are also made of steel.

One of the main disadvantages of iron and steel is that they rust if exposed to moisture and air. 'Tin' cans are made of steel that is coated with a very thin layer of another metal, tin, to prevent it from rusting.

TEST FILE

HARDER METALS

With the supervision of an adult, gather together some old, unwanted metal items. These might be a fork or spoon, some large paper clips, a small saucepan, a screwdriver, a food can, a drink can and a rasp or file. See how the metals differ in hardness. Try scratching each item with all the others. Make a table of the results showing which item is the softest, being marked by all the others, and which is hardest, scratching all the others but hardly being marked itself. Consider how the hardness is linked to the item's use. For example, a rasp or file is designed to rub or abrade other materials so it has to be very hard.

PRECIOUS AND SPECIAL METALS

Bracelets and necklaces made of iron or tin are not very valuable. But those made from gold, silver and similar precious metals have been desired through history. These metals are among the most precious natural resources for various reasons. One is that, like precious stones, they are scarce in Earth's crust. So possessing them shows a person has wealth or power. Coins have also been made from precious metals, so that they not only represent wealth, but are valuable themselves.

Most precious metals are also valuable because they are tough, long-lasting, do not corrode, and have attractive features such as a beautiful colour and lustre, or shine. They can also be worked or shaped into delicate designs.

Shaping history

Some precious metals have affected history. During gold rushes, people race to an area where gold ores or nuggets are found to seek their fortunes. This has happened in California in North America, the Amazon in South America and the outback of Australia.

Scientists devise new combinations of rare metals for certain tasks, such as carrying electricity almost perfectly in new types of superconductors.

Since ancient times gold has been valued for its colour and shine. It is also tough, long-lasting, hardly corrodes and yet is easily shaped.

Gold and silver have modern practical uses, too. Silver is one of the best conductors of electricity and is suited to very delicate electrical circuits. Certain chemicals containing silver are altered and become darker when exposed to light. These light-sensitive, silver-containing chemicals are used in photographic film. Gold's resistance to corrosion and ability to carry electricity well makes it ideal for micro-switches in computers and other electronic equipment.

The new precious metals

As technology progresses, other rare metals have become precious for their scientific and industrial uses. Some are worth more, weight for weight, than gold.

The Northrop B-2 'stealth bomber' is made from about 120 different metals and alloys (metal mixtures), each doing one precise job.

FUTURE FILE

METALS FROM SPACE?

There are limited supplies of precious metals here on Earth. Extracting them from their ores is a long, costly and complicated process. It can also produce much waste and pollution. Space research shows that some of these metals are present on other planets. Perhaps spacecraft in the future will travel to other worlds, mine the rocks there, obtain the precious metals and bring them back to Earth.

For example palladium, platinum and rhodium are used in vehicle CATs (catalytic converters) that reduce pollution from exhaust fumes.

Titanium is a tough and common metal. (It is the ninth most abundant element in Earth's crust.) Titanium is difficult to purify from its ores, because it is very hard and resistant to heat. However, these features also make it ideal for use in rockets, high-speed aircraft, jet engines and racing cars.

Danger from metals

Some metals are harmful to living things, including people – especially if they are breathed in or consumed in food or drink. Several of these are called **heavy metals** because they are indeed heavy, dense substances. They include mercury and cadmium, which are used to make certain types of electrical batteries. These should always be disposed of carefully to prevent them from leaking into soil or water where they cause pollution.

FOSSIL FUELS – OIL AND GAS

What do a truck's diesel fuel, its plastic steering wheel, the paint on its cab and the lubricating oil in its engine have in common with each other – and with the tarmac road underneath? They are all made from petroleum, commonly called crude oil or oil.

In the 20th century the natural resource of oil came to dominate the world's industries, businesses and even politics. It is so valuable that it is called 'black gold'. Oil shortages can trigger strikes and revolutions. Wars have been fought over it. However, oil is a non-renewable resource so it is certain to become more scarce in the future.

How oil formed

Oil, natural gas and coal (see page 30) are fossil fuels. They were formed over millions of years from the remains of once-living things. Oil and natural gas began as tiny plants and animals that once lived in the sea. They died and sank to form a layer of mud on the seabed.

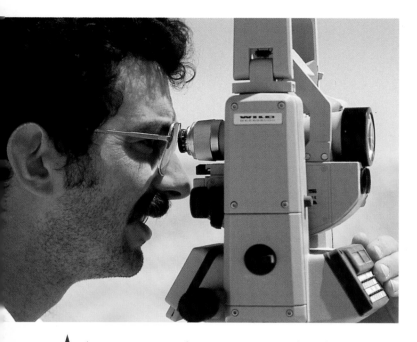

A surveyor taking accurate land measurements in preparation for a seismic survey to search for oil.

The world's known oil reserves. Oil has formed during most of Earth's history. About one-half of the current known oil fields are in the Middle East region.

Over millions of years the soft mud was squeezed, heated and cemented to form rock. The pressure and warmth, about 80–100°C, turned the decaying remains of the tiny plants and animals into a thick, dark, sticky liquid – oil. This seeped through the rocks to collect in pools. Oil droplets filled the gaps between rock particles like water in a sponge. This is the oil that people drill for today.

Natural gas formed in a similar way to oil, as a result of the remains of living things decaying. It often collected like a large bubble in the spongy rock above an oil pool. In most places the oil and gas are kept below the surface by layers of solid rocks above them, which they cannot seep through. Here and there oil reaches the surface where it forms thick, tarry pools.

A small, mobile drill rig takes samples of soil for later study. The types of mineral particles can help to identify the rocks deep below the surface.

 **FACT FILE**

OIL – WHERE AND WHEN
Petroleum oil has formed during most time spans, or **geological periods**, during Earth's very long history. The main periods are the Ordovician (505–430 million years ago), Devonian (410–360), Carboniferous (360–280), Permian (280–245), Cretaceous (144–65) and Tertiary (65–2) periods.

The main oil fields in the world are in the Middle East, which has over half of the estimated **reserves**. There are also major oil fields in West Africa, North Africa, the North Sea, the Gulf of Mexico, Alaska and western Siberia.

The search for oil
Striking oil in a region brings great wealth, so many countries actively search for this valuable natural resource. Scientists use various survey methods (see page 14). In particular, small explosions or thumper machines are used to send shock waves through the ground. The waves are affected in different ways by different types of rocks deep below the surface, revealing rocks that may contain oil.

If an oil or gas field seems likely, test boreholes are drilled at various sites in the area to check the size and depth of the field before oil production starts, as explained on page 26.

OIL DRILLS AND RIGS

Oil and gas are found under the ground and below the seabed. They are usually reached by drilling. A drill rig or platform has a tall tower called a derrick. This holds the drill pipes that are joined end to end to make a 'pipe string' which is lengthened as the hole deepens.

The modern drill

In older drill systems the whole pipe string, which could be over 5,000 metres long, spins around. It turns the toothed, diamond-tipped cutting bit at its tip which bores through the rock. In modern drill systems only the bit spins around while the main pipe string stays still. The bit, which is slightly wider than the drill string, is turned by a mud mixture pumped down the inside of the hollow pipe string. The mud forces its way through a spiral-shaped motor just behind the tip that makes the bit twist. The mud then flows out at the bit, flushes away pieces of rubbed-off rock, and carries them back up the hole.

In the North Sea a huge oil rig platform burns off waste gases.

Steering the drill

The modern drill is computer-controlled and steerable. The bit can be set at a slight angle to the pipe string just behind it, so it cuts a curved path. The sections of pipe in the string follow the curve. Twisting the whole pipe string from the surface turns the angled bit so that it cuts in a different direction. In this way the bit, pulling the pipe string behind it, can turn a right-angle corner in less than 100 metres and then drill straight again. It can even head back up towards the surface.

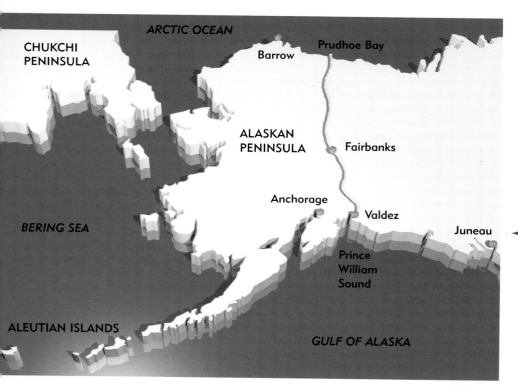

ARCTIC OCEAN

CHUKCHI PENINSULA

Barrow

Prudhoe Bay

ALASKAN PENINSULA

Fairbanks

Anchorage

Valdez

Juneau

Prince William Sound

BERING SEA

ALEUTIAN ISLANDS

GULF OF ALASKA

The trans-Alaska pipeline carries oil across remote north-west North America. Giant oil tankers then take the oil to the big refineries farther south.

Into production

Oil and gas may be a few metres down, or more than 5,000 metres below the surface, where rock temperatures are 200°C. About one-third of the world's oil comes from under the seabed. Wells have been drilled into the bed under shallow seas, from a ship or platform, for many years. Recent advances allow wells to be bored into the ocean floor, which is itself 2,000 metres below the surface.

Once the test bores are completed, a production rig and pipes are installed and the oil can flow. It may come out under its own pressure or be forced out by 'nodding donkey' pumps. The oil is then sent along a pipeline, or stored in large holding tanks and taken away regularly by an oil tanker ship, to its destination – the petroleum refinery.

An oil supertanker being docked by tug boats. Its cargo of crude oil will be pumped out through pipelines into storage tanks.

HISTORY FILE

THE OIL BUSINESS
- **1859** The first oil well was drilled at Titusville, Pennsylvania, USA. This was the beginning of oil as big business.
- **1908** Oil found in west Asia, especially in Persia (now Iran).
- **Early 1930s** Discoveries of large oil fields in Texas, USA.
- **Late 1930s** Oil found in Middle East.
- **1967** Oil reserves located in Prudhoe Bay, Alaska (see opposite).
- **1970s** The former Soviet Union (Russia and neighbouring countries) became the largest oil producers.
- **1990s** Oil fields exploited in Siberia.
- **2000** Petrol shortage in UK caused by people protesting against high fuel prices.

The Gulf War of 1991 in the Middle East was partly triggered by disputes over oil fields in Kuwait, where hundreds of wells were set ablaze.

PETROCHEMICALS

Oil (crude oil or petroleum) is probably Earth's most adaptable and most widely used natural resource. It is a complex mixture of many substances. These are the basis of one of the world's biggest industries, the petrochemical industry. First the crude oil must be treated and split up into its many parts. This process is called refining and is carried out at oil refineries, which are some of the largest industrial sites on Earth.

Separating the fractions

Most oil refineries have sets of very tall towers called distillation columns. The crude oil is heated and its substances turn into gases. The gases rise in the tower and become cooler with height. Each type of gas cools and condenses (turns back into a liquid) at a certain temperature and height in the column.

The substances obtained at these levels are called **fractions**. The lighter ones remain as gases or condense into runny liquids near the top of the tower. The heavier, thicker ones condense lower down. The whole process is called fractional distillation.

Cracking the fractions

Some of the oil fractions are further refined by 'cracking'. They are treated with heat and chemicals called **catalysts**, to split them apart and recombine them into yet more products. Refining and cracking generally yield the following products, from lightest to heaviest:

- Chemical solvents.
- Very light liquid fuels such as paraffin.
- Petrol (gasoline) and fuels for jet and propeller planes.

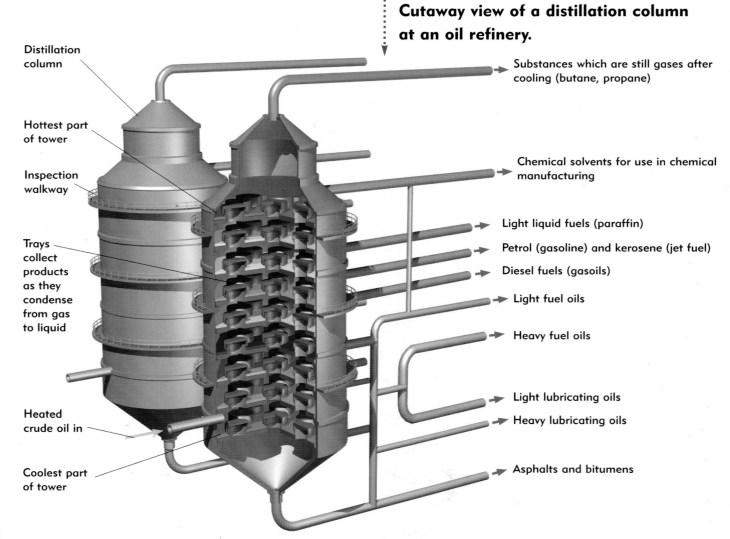

Cutaway view of a distillation column at an oil refinery.

Distillation column

Hottest part of tower

Inspection walkway

Trays collect products as they condense from gas to liquid

Heated crude oil in

Coolest part of tower

Substances which are still gases after cooling (butane, propane)

Chemical solvents for use in chemical manufacturing

Light liquid fuels (paraffin)

Petrol (gasoline) and kerosene (jet fuel)

Diesel fuels (gasoils)

Light fuel oils

Heavy fuel oils

Light lubricating oils

Heavy lubricating oils

Asphalts and bitumens

Hundreds of pipes, carrying the products from oil refining, dwarf a worker who turns one of the valves (taps) to adjust the flow.

- Diesel fuels (gasoils) for trucks and locomotives.
- Light fuel oils for burning in heating systems.
- Heavy fuel oils for burning in power stations and ships.
- Light lubricating oils for hand tools, sewing machines and similar equipment.
- Heavy lubricating oils for cars, trucks and other large machinery.
- Asphalts and bitumens for road surfacing.

More oil products

The products from crude oil include many chemicals used in industry. They include hundreds of kinds of plastics, artificial rubbers, artificial fibres for clothes and textiles, paints and **pigments** (coloured substances) and many kinds of waxes.

The upper layers of a modern road, including bituminous asphalt and thick tar, are some of the thousands of products obtained from oil.

 FACT FILE

RECYCLE!

Because oil is a non-renewable resource, existing supplies will eventually run out (see page 42). This is why it is important to recycle, or collect and use again, oil products such as plastics. Then they do not have to be made from new supplies of oil. Recycling saves time and energy as well as raw materials. It helps even more if plastics are sorted into their different types for recycling.
- **ABS** Acrylic butadiene styrene nitrile, used for plastic pipes, sheets, strong casings, crates and car parts.
- **PET** Polyethylene terephthalate, used mainly to make fizzy drink bottles.
- **PVC** Polyvinyl chloride, used in other drink bottles, food trays and blister packaging.

Coal was formed from the remains of plants that lived millions of years ago. It is one of the most valuable and widely used natural resources. Like oil, coal is a fossil fuel that is burned to produce heat. Coal is also a non-renewable resource (see page 9).

How coal formed

Millions of years ago in marshes and swamps, plants thrived and died. They were soon covered by more plants. The dead remains partly decayed and were squashed as they were buried deeper. They formed a brown, spongy substance called peat. As the pressure and heat increased, water was squeezed out of the peat and the remains became harder, heavier and darker. The process continued to form different substances at each stage – peat, lignite, coal and anthracite (see Fact File).

FACT FILE

TYPES OF COAL
- Lignite (brown coal) generally formed when plant remains were buried to a depth of about 1,000 metres.
- Bituminous coal, the familiar type burned in homes, formed at depths of about 3,000 metres.
- Anthracite formed at depths of about 6,000 metres under intense heat and pressure.

All three of these substances can be mined and burned as fuel. For the same-sized lump of each, lignite gives out least heat but gives off most smoke and other polluting substances, while anthracite produces most heat and produces little smoke or polluting substances.

A cutaway view of a deep coal mine.

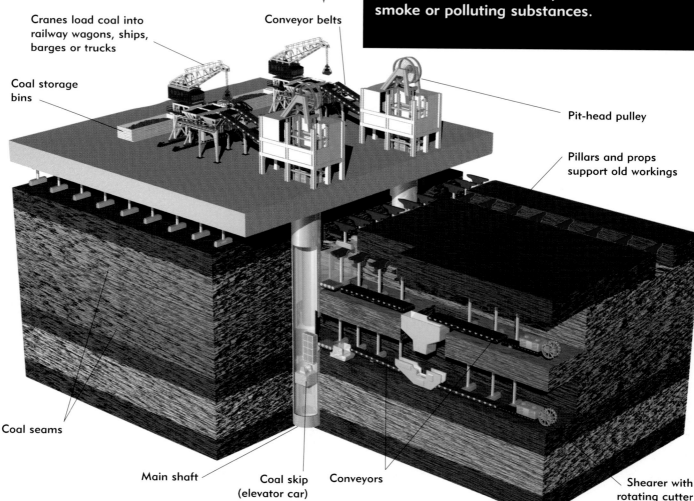

Cranes load coal into railway wagons, ships, barges or trucks

Conveyor belts

Coal storage bins

Pit-head pulley

Pillars and props support old workings

Coal seams

Main shaft

Coal skip (elevator car)

Conveyors

Shearer with rotating cutter

A technician checks noise safety levels near a large, many-bladed shearer which slices coal onto a roller conveyor.

Coal-fired power stations burn mountains of coal, brought by railway or ship, to convert the chemical energy that the coal contains into heat and then to electricity.

Coal at the surface

Coal at or just below Earth's surface is scraped up by huge machines, a process known as open-cast or strip mining. In former times these mines were left as giant scars on the landscape. Today in some areas, surface soil is removed first and stored. After the coal is extracted the soil is replaced and trees are planted to try and restore the natural habitat.

Mining deeper coal

There are many ways of mining coal. Sometimes the layers or seams run into a hillside, and a drift mine follows them inwards. A slope mine can follow the coal seam downwards from the surface. In a shaft mine people and equipment are lowered down lift-type shafts to the depth of the seams. Once in the coal seam, the coal can be broken up with explosives (see page 16) or by massive chainsaws or circular-saw undercutters. The coal is crumbled onto a conveyor belt or into trucks and transported to the surface.

Coal products

Coal can be burned as a fuel. It can also be processed and cracked, much like oil, to make various products:
• Coal gases for burning.
• Solvents for the chemical industry.
• Naphthalene for pigments, dyes, lubricants and various fungus- and insect-repellents. (It gives the smell to mothballs.)
• Creosote, the strong-smelling wood preservative.
• Coal tar pitch, for use in chemical processes, furnaces and as a protective covering on roofs and walls.

Most of the world's remaining coal fields are in China, Russia and North America. There are also fields in Europe, India, Australia and South America.

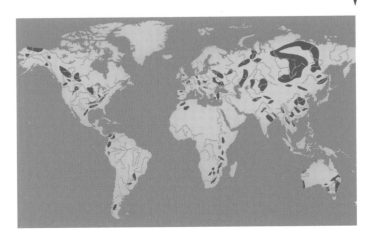

BIO-RESOURCES

More than four-fifths of all energy used in the world today is obtained by burning the fossil fuels coal, gas and oil. Half of the remaining energy used in the world comes from burning wood and wood products, especially in less developed countries. Firewood supplies warmth, light and heat for cooking. This shows the importance of wood as a natural resource for energy. Like oil, gas and coal, wood is a **bio-resource**. This means it is derived from living things.

Types of wood

Two main types of trees yield two groups of wood. Conifer (cone-bearing) trees such as pines, spruces, firs, larches and redwoods produce softwoods. Hardwoods come from blossom or flower-producing trees such as oak, ash, elm, beech, maple, hickory, eucalypts (gums), mahogany and teak.

Wood is not only an energy-yielding resource. It is also used to make innumerable items and structures, from utensils such as bowls and spoons to log cabins and bridges. It is also sliced or shredded and treated to make paper, card and boards such as hardboards and chipboards.

Oil-seed rape, also known as colza or canola, yields an oil which can be used for cooking, to lubricate machines and as a fuel for engines and heating systems.

Collecting firewood can take several hours each day in rural areas, where many nearby trees have already been cut down.

Sustainable use

In most parts of the developed world new forests are planted, mainly of softwoods, to replace trees that are cut down. This practice, where the old trees are replaced by new ones, is known as **sustainable** use. In some countries the trees, especially certain tropical hardwoods like teak and mahogany, are cut down without being replaced. This non-sustainable use destroys whole areas of rare forest habitat.

Other bio-resources

Certain bio-resources are essential for survival. These are the plant crops and farm animals that provide food for people and other living things. Plant crops are grown for other uses, too. Cotton, flax and hemp yield natural fibres which are used for making clothes, ropes and other products.

Bio-fuels are plants, plant products or animal products which can be burned to provide heat energy for cooking, warmth or generating electricity (see page 34). They include the 'supergrass' miscanthus, the coba tree and the gopher plant, and plant oils extracted from corn (maize), sunflower, olive and oil-seed rape. Cars and trucks can be made to run on these plant-based bio-fuels.

As plant and animal matter decays, as in a compost heap, it produces flammable, energy-containing gases such as methane. These can be collected in bio-digesters and burned in small-scale electricity generators, cookers and vehicle engines.

Hardwood logs wait at a sawmill in Central America.

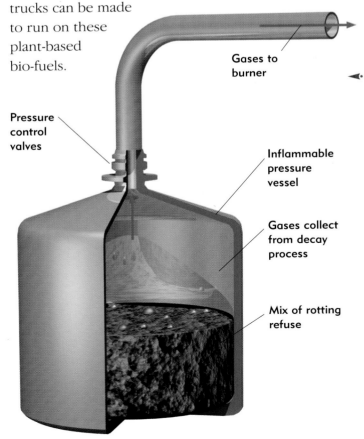

Pressure control valves

Gases to burner

Inflammable pressure vessel

Gases collect from decay process

Mix of rotting refuse

In a bio-digester, rotting refuse produces gases which can be burnt as fuel.

TEST FILE

SUSTAINABLE TIMBER

Visit your local timber merchant or wood store. Check the information given about the origins of the different types of wood. Look for labels and schemes that advertise sustainable or renewable sources of wood, where forests are replanted. Does the store have a leaflet explaining that it supports schemes for sustainable timber?

RESOURCES FOR ELECTRICITY

Waste steam escapes into the cold air like white smoke from the Nesjavellir geothermal power station in Iceland.

Huge amounts of Earth's natural resources are used to generate electricity. Electricity is widely used because it is very adaptable. It can be sent long distances along wires and cables, and turned into heat, light, movement and sound. Most electricity is generated by burning fossil fuels, which are non-renewable. At today's rate of use the known reserves of coal, oil and gas will run out in less than 200 years. In addition, burning these fuels in electricity generating stations causes pollution and damages the environment (see page 15).

New approaches

One approach to help solve this problem is to develop natural resources for generating electricity that are sustainable and which cause much less pollution and environmental damage. Many such energy sources are available, as shown on the following pages. Additional approaches include making electricity power stations more efficient, and encouraging people, businesses and industries to be more careful about wasting electricity.

In older power stations like this one, some of the energy produced is wasted in the form of steam. Newer power stations use this energy to heat the buildings.

FACT FILE

ENERGY TO ELECTRICITY

In general, industrialized countries generate electricity from these various sources:
- Burning coal 44%
- Burning natural gas 17%
- Burning oil 12%
- Nuclear fuel 9%
- Hydroelectric power (from running water) 11%
- Burning bio-fuels such as wood, plant oils and vegetable rubbish 3%
- Wind, solar, geothermal, tidal and other energy sources 4%

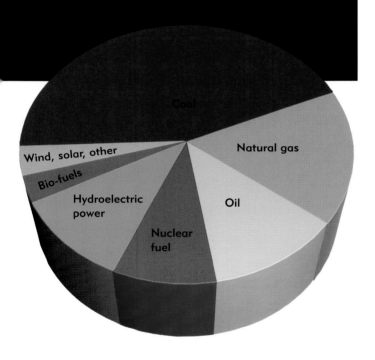

France built many nuclear power stations, like this one at Creys-Malville. Some countries have avoided this type of energy for electricity generation.

At present there is no long-term way of dealing with these radioactive products and wastes. There is also the possibility of a nuclear accident which could kill many people and pollute large areas with radioactivity. In some regions nuclear power is now being phased out.

Geothermal energy

Another energy resource is heat from rocks deep inside Earth. This is known as geothermal energy. In some regions, such as Iceland and New Zealand, water trickles down through cracks in the rocks, is heated into steam, expands and bursts up to the surface as natural hot springs or geysers. These can be tapped to provide heat energy that warms homes and other buildings or generates electricity. Holes can be drilled deep into hot rocks and water pumped down to carry the heat back up.

Geothermal energy causes no pollution and is renewable for the foreseeable future. It costs large amounts of money to construct the equipment for obtaining it, but after this, the costs are much lower. However only certain regions of the world have suitably hot rocks near the surface.

Nuclear energy

Nuclear energy involves splitting nuclei – the central parts of atoms, which are the smallest parts of a substance. As the nuclei split they give off large amounts of heat energy which can be converted into electricity. One of the main nuclear fuels is uranium, a metal obtained by mining. However uranium, and the products it forms after it is used as fuel, are radioactive. They give off invisible rays and particles that can damage and kill living things. Some of the radioactivity will last for thousands of years.

POWER FROM WATER

Movement is a type of energy called kinetic energy. Moving water represents an energy source. Since ancient times it has been harnessed by watermills to drive machinery. A modern version of the watermill is the hydroelectric power station. It changes the energy of flowing water into electricity.

A hydroelectric power station is expensive to build and can cause drastic changes to the environment. However, once it is established it uses no fuel, causes no air pollution and has low running costs. Some countries with many fast-flowing rivers, such as Norway, Canada and New Zealand, obtain most of their electricity in this way. Most other countries have few such rivers and cannot develop this type of energy source.

The dam and lake

A typical hydroelectric power station has a large wall, the dam, across a river. This makes the water build up into an artificial lake. The lake evens out water flow through the seasons so the power station works efficiently all year round. In addition, water from the lake can be piped or channelled to surrounding farmland to help crops grow.

Inside the power station

Water flows through pipes inside the dam and past turbines, which are like large fans with angled blades. The surging water makes the turbines spin around with great force. The central shafts of the turbines are connected to electricity generators as in other types of power stations.

Hydroelectric problems

Hydroelectricity generation can cause problems. The lake that forms behind the dam floods vast areas of land. Whole villages and towns may 'drown' and the people have to move. Rare animals, plants and habitats may be destroyed. Fish and other animals may no longer be able to migrate along the river. Also the changed flow of the river may mean less water downstream for crops and people there. Another problem is that mud and silt normally carried along by the river may build up behind the dam and gradually clog up rivers and waterways.

The world's only tidal power station is at the mouth of the River Rance, in northern France. Its wall-like barrage is also a crossing for vehicles.

FACT FILE

BIG HYDRO-POWER SCHEMES

• The Itaipu hydroelectric scheme is the world's biggest power producer. It is a group of power stations on the Paraná River between Paraguay and Brazil. It produces 13,300 megawatts. (A very large coal-fired or nuclear power station produces 4,000–5,000 megawatts, enough for a country half the size of Denmark.)

• In about 2009 the Three Gorges Dam and hydroelectric scheme in China should rival Itaipu. The dam will be 2,300 metres long, 183 metres high and have 26 giant turbines and generators. The lake behind the Three Gorges Dam will have an area of more than 600 square kilometres.

The incredible energy of rushing water is shown by this power surge at the Itaipu hydroelectric scheme in South America.

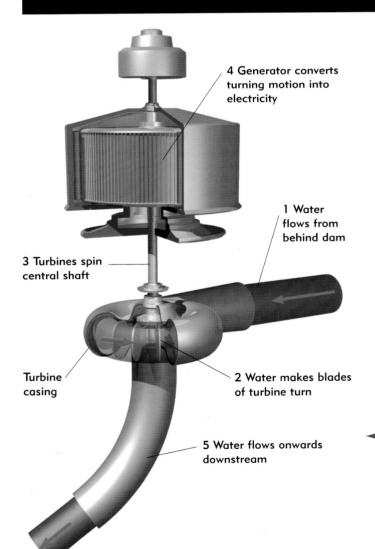

4 Generator converts turning motion into electricity

1 Water flows from behind dam

3 Turbines spin central shaft

Turbine casing

2 Water makes blades of turbine turn

5 Water flows onwards downstream

During the 19th century factories such as cotton mills were built near fast rivers, partly so the energy of flowing water could drive machinery.

Inside a dam, water turns turbine blades and the turning motion is then converted into electricity by generators.

WIND, WAVES AND TIDES

In the same way that moving water is an energy source, so is moving air – wind. Since ancient times people have used wind power in windmills and sailing ships. The modern version of the windmill is the aerogenerator or wind turbine. The wind spins its large, fan-like rotor blades which are connected to a generator to produce electricity. Several aerogenerators together in a windy place are known as a wind farm.

The modern aerogenerator is largely automatic and controlled by a computer. It swivels around so that it always faces the wind for maximum efficiency. Its blades can alter their angle of tilt so they work well in different wind speeds. They can even be held still, so they do not spin too fast and shatter in storm winds.

Windy limits

Like hydroelectric power stations, aerogenerators harness a sustainable or renewable energy source. Once completed, their running costs are low and they produce no air or soil pollution.

A drawback of aerogenerators is that they are costly to design and build. Also, to give a worthwhile and steady output of electricity, they must be built in areas where winds are strong and reliable. These are often in high areas like mountain passes or flat coastlines, far from the cities where most of the electricity is used. This requires very long power lines to carry the electricity long distances across the countryside. Also aerogenerators can cause 'visual pollution', ruining the view in areas of great natural beauty. They may also frighten away animals or harm birds that fly too near.

Wave and tidal power

As winds blow over seas they create waves. The moving water in waves is another natural source of energy which could be tapped. There have been dozens of test designs for devices to change wave energy into electrical power. But there are many practical problems. Waves vary greatly with the weather so the output of electricity is irregular, and storms can damage the machinery.

Osprey 1 was a machine designed to generate electricity from the energy in sea waves. It was launched in 1995 but failed after a few weeks.

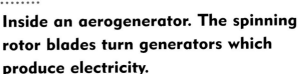

This wind farm in Tehachepi, California covers more land area than any other collection of aerogenerators (wind turbines) in the world.

FUTURE FILE

A WIND-POWERED COUNTRY

In 1998 Denmark announced a plan to produce half of the electricity it needs – about 5,500 megawatts – using wind power by the year 2030. This means adding to its 4,000 existing small aerogenerators, starting with 500 new large ones generating 750 megawatts by 2008. Most of these new wind farms will be built in remote, shallow-water coastal areas, where people are unlikely to complain about 'visual pollution' and where the winds are strong and steady.

Inside an aerogenerator. The spinning rotor blades turn generators which produce electricity.

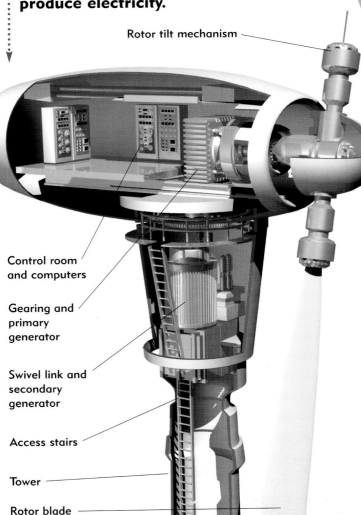

Rotor tilt mechanism

Control room and computers

Gearing and primary generator

Swivel link and secondary generator

Access stairs

Tower

Rotor blade

Another form of moving water is the rise and fall of the tide. Its energy can be harnessed by a dam-like wall or barrage across a river mouth or inlet where the tide rises and falls by a large amount. The barrage works like a two-way hydroelectric power station (see page 36). As the tide comes in and goes out, water flows through turbines in the barrage and spins them to produce electricity.

Tidal power is regular and sustainable and produces no obvious pollution. However, as with wave energy, this type of power station is very costly to build. It is subject to damage from storms and large waves. Sea water is corrosive and rusts or ruins the machinery. The barrage can also alter the coastline and threaten important natural habitats such as mudflats.

ENERGY FROM THE SUN

nergy from the Sun, or solar energy, is not really one of Earth's own resources. But it is available for use on Earth after its 8-minute, 150-million-kilometre journey through space. The energy is in two main forms, light and heat. It is the most sustainable resource available – the Sun should shine continuously for another 4,000 million years or so.

A Sun-powered world

There are several ways of trapping and using solar energy directly, and of converting it into electricity. Indeed, in one sense, the world is already solar-powered. As explained on previous pages, bio-resources such as coal, oil and wood are obtained from plants that grew by trapping light energy from the Sun, in the process of photosynthesis (see page 11). As they burn, bio-fuels release energy that came originally from the Sun.

Almost the whole roofs of these houses are covered with solar cells in this test project in Heerhugowaard, Netherlands.

This solar furnace at Font Romeu in the Pyrenees Mountains of France has large curved mirrors to concentrate the Sun's heat rays.

The Sun's light

Devices that convert light energy directly into electricity are called solar cells. One cell produces a tiny amount of electricity, perhaps enough to work a pocket calculator. Thousands of cells connected together on a large panel make much more electricity, enough to be useful in a house. A solar electricity generating station has thousands of these solar panels. The largest is the Harper Lake site in the Mojave Desert, USA. Its 520 hectares of panels generate 160 megawatts of electricity.

At present, solar cells have many limitations. They are only about 20 per cent efficient, which means they change one-fifth of the light energy they receive into electricity. Also, sunlight is not a very strong or concentrated type of energy so the resulting amounts of electricity are small. The cells are costly to make and work only where and when the Sun shines brightly.

Solar panels such as those on the Hubble Space Telescope, here being released from the space shuttle, convert sunlight directly into electricity.

FUTURE FILE

THE SOLAR CHIMNEY

A design for a new type of solar power station is the solar chimney. It would be built in a hot, sunny place like a desert. It has a huge, flat glass roof a couple of metres above the ground, like a greenhouse but is open around the sides, with a tall chimney at the centre. As the Sun heats the air and ground, hot air rises powerfully up the chimney and spins aerogenerator-like wind turbines there to generate electricity.

A planned solar chimney in Transvaal, South Africa, will have a chimney 1,500 metres tall and a glass collector 7 kilometres across. It should generate 200 megawatts and cost £250 million. Once built it would tap sustainable energy and be almost maintenance-free.

The Sun's heat

Small, door-sized solar panels that collect the Sun's heat are becoming more common on the roofs of homes and other buildings. Most designs contain tubes through which a gas or liquid passes. The tubes may be glass or metal and are designed to absorb the Sun's heat. The flowing liquid or gas collects the heat and takes it into the building, usually to make hot water. The system works well in sunny weather but it needs another 'top-up' source of heat in cloudy conditions or during the long nights of winter. A solar furnace gathers the Sun's heat using many mirrors that reflect the heat rays onto a central collector. The concentrated heat is used to generate electricity. The solar furnace at Barstow, California, USA has more than 1,800 heat-focusing mirrors.

CAN EARTH SURVIVE?

As people use Earth's natural resources, we may seem only to scratch the surface of the planet. Yet, in many cases the resources will not last if we continue using them at the present rate. Predictions for how long oil reserves will last vary from 40 to about 200 years. Coal may last slightly longer, but not much.

Some scientists believe that fuel cells may provide cheap, clean energy for the future. In a fuel cell electricity is made when oxygen and hydrogen react to produce electricity and water.

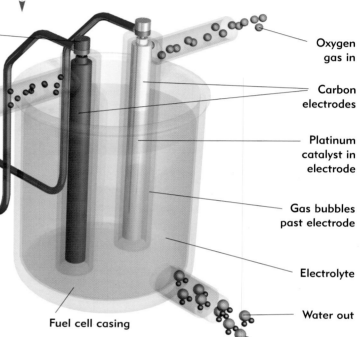

Electrodes gather electric current

Hydrogen gas in

Electricity drives motor

Oxygen gas in

Carbon electrodes

Platinum catalyst in electrode

Gas bubbles past electrode

Electrolyte

Water out

Fuel cell casing

In addition, the burning of fossil fuels causes environmental problems such as air, soil and water pollution, smog and acid rain, and also contributes to global warming and loss of ozone.

Byker power station, north-east England, burns household rubbish to make electricity and also heat local buildings including 1,700 homes.

Changing demand

Added to this problem is the fact that our use of Earth's resources is rising. During the 1990s global demand for oil rose at 2 per cent each year. In some areas the demand was steady or even fell as people adopted energy-saving measures such as smaller cars, better use of public transport, more recycling and more efficient insulation in buildings. But this fall was outweighed by rocketing demand in other regions. Between the years 1985 and 2000 demand for energy rose by 30 per cent in parts of South America, 40 per cent in Africa and almost 50 per cent in some regions of Asia.

These huge rises in demand for energy resources are linked to increasing demand for material resources, especially metals such as iron and aluminium and the plastics produced from oil. These materials supply huge factories that manufacture cars, washing machines, computers and other consumer goods.

Instead of filling up with petrol, electric cars plug in at Sacramento, California. Their batteries recharge with electricity direct from solar panels.

 **FACT FILE**

RECYCLING EARTH'S RESOURCES
Recycling (see page 29) is one of the main actions needed for the future.
• World-wide more than 50 per cent of the steel produced today is made from recycled scrap iron and steel. Compared to making new steel, this cuts down the energy needed by 75 per cent. It also reduces scarring of the landscape by open-cast or surface mining for iron ore.
• In countries such as Sweden, up to 90 per cent of supplies of the metal aluminium come from recycled items such as drink cans. Using this recycled aluminium saves up to 90 per cent of the energy used to make new aluminium.

Hope for the future

Earth is huge but many of its natural resources are limited. They cannot be plundered forever. Resources must be both conserved and recycled.

Individual people can make a difference by using electricity, heat and other forms of energy carefully, by conserving resources like food and water, and by supporting recycling schemes. People can also put pressure on their local and national governments, for example, to expand research into sustainable sources of energy and increase renewable supplies of timber. Power stations can be made more efficient and industries less wasteful.

The problems mounting now, as we use and waste Earth's natural resources, will have to be tackled at some time. Otherwise the young people of today may be left to suffer the consequences in the future.

Giant holes scar the landscape at this 1960s open-cast coal mine in Arizona. In newer mines some of the original surface soil and wildlife are replaced.

GLOSSARY AND FURTHER INFO

Acid rain Rain which has taken in polluting acidic or corrosive substances from the atmosphere.

Bio-resource A resource in the form of a living thing or obtained from a living thing.

Catalysts Substances which speed up or slow down chemical changes, without changing themselves.

Corrode To break down or wear away, especially by strong chemicals such as acids.

Element A single, pure chemical substance which cannot be broken down by ordinary chemical means into any simpler substances.

Fertile When a soil is rich in minerals, nutrients and other substances and supports plentiful plant growth.

Fractions Different single substances or ingredients obtained from a mixture or combination.

Gems Valuable mineral substances which have been cut, shaped and polished for great beauty.

Geological period One of the very long time spans in the history of Earth, identified mainly from the types of rocks formed during it.

Heavy metals Metals (see below) which are dense or heavy, and which can cause great harm to living things even in tiny amounts.

Humus The usually brown, crumbly upper layer of soil, rich in the rotting or decaying remains of plants and animals.

Metals Pure chemical elements (see above) which are usually tough, hard and shiny, and which carry heat and electricity well.

Microbes Tiny living things which can only be seen with the aid of a microscope.

Nutrients Substances which living things need to take in, to survive and grow and stay healthy.

Open-cast mining When minerals are obtained at or near Earth's surface, usually from a large hole.

Photosynthesis When plants use the energy in sunlight to join carbon dioxide gas (from air) and water to form energy-rich foods such as sugars.

Pigments Coloured substances in paints and dyes.

Recycle To use something or part of it again, rather than to make a new one.

Reserves Unused or remaining amounts.

Sustainable When a substance or process can continue in the future, without running out.

PLACES TO VISIT

Natural History Museum
Cromwell Road, London SW7 5BD
Web site: www.nhm.ac.uk/museum
Earth galleries (formerly the Geology Museum) include many exhibitions on rocks, minerals, fossils.

Ashmolean Museum of Art and Archaeology
Beaumont Street, Oxford OX1 2PH
Displays on earth minerals, rocks and resources.

National Coal Mining Museum
New Road, Overton, Wakefield, WF4 4RH
Web site: www.ncm.org.uk
Includes a trip 130 metres down one of the oldest working mines in England.

BOOKS TO READ

The World's Mineral Resources by Robin Kerrod (Thomson Learning, 1994)
Ecology: Earth's Living Resources by Anthea Maton (Prentice Hall School Group, 1997)
Gemstones by Christine Woodward (Sterling Publications, 1988)
Geothermal and Bio-Energy (Energy Forever) by Ian Graham (Raintree/Steck Vaughn, 1999)

WEB SITES

British Geological Survey Home Page
www.bgs.ac.uk
The British Geological Survey (BGS) collects and analyses much of the nation's geological, mineral and related scientific information.

Institute of Petroleum: Energy for the World
www.petroleum.co.uk/energy.htm
Educational resource provided by the Institute of Petroleum (61 New Cavendish Street, London W1M) for a wide variety of petrochemical-linked subjects.

The Virtual Earth
teachserv.earth.ox.ac.uk/resources/v_earth.html
A tour of the World Wide Web for earth scientists showing how to use the Web to gather information.

INDEX

How Glass is Made

Typical glass is made from sand (silica), soda (sodium carbonate), limestone and other minerals including cullet (recycled glass). These are ground up, mixed and heated to about 1,300°C to make the glass molten and runny. In the float glass process, a ribbon of liquid glass is floated on a bath of the molten metal tin, whose shiny surface gives the glass an amazingly smooth finish.

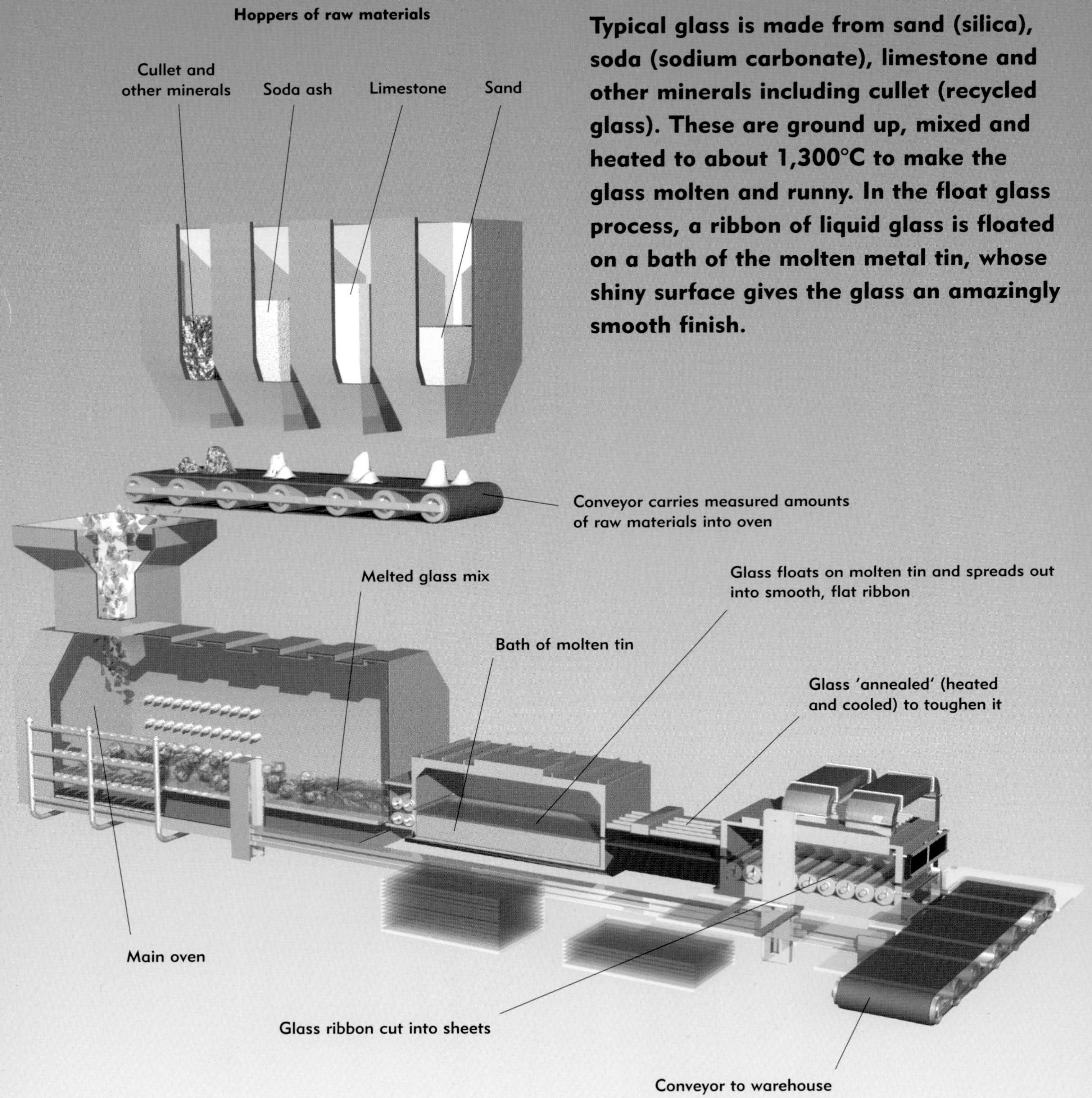

Hoppers of raw materials

Cullet and other minerals

Soda ash

Limestone

Sand

Conveyor carries measured amounts of raw materials into oven

Melted glass mix

Glass floats on molten tin and spreads out into smooth, flat ribbon

Bath of molten tin

Glass 'annealed' (heated and cooled) to toughen it

Main oven

Glass ribbon cut into sheets

Conveyor to warehouse

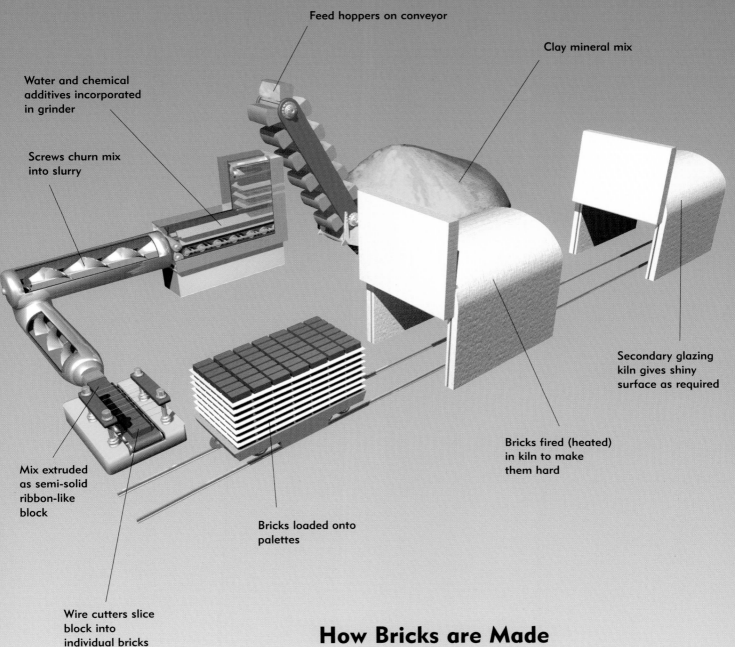

Feed hoppers on conveyor

Clay mineral mix

Water and chemical additives incorporated in grinder

Screws churn mix into slurry

Mix extruded as semi-solid ribbon-like block

Wire cutters slice block into individual bricks

Bricks loaded onto palettes

Bricks fired (heated) in kiln to make them hard

Secondary glazing kiln gives shiny surface as required

How Bricks are Made

Bricks and tiles are made from clay minerals, perhaps mixed with shale, then put into moulds or sliced into box-like shapes. They are hardened by heat in a kiln, called firing.